SUMO
SHOWDOWN

THE HAWAIIAN CHALLENGE

SUMO
SHOWDOWN

THE HAWAIIAN CHALLENGE

Philip Sandoz

CHARLES E. TUTTLE COMPANY

Rutland, Vermont & Tokyo, Japan

PHOTOS:
(p. 1) Yobidashi (beckoners) sweep the dohyo during a basho
at Tokyo's Kokugikan.
(pp. 2–3) Interior view of the Kokugikan, where three tournaments
are held annually.
(p. 4) Crowds gather to watch the rikishis' banners at Tokyo's Kokugikan.

Published by the Charles E. Tuttle Company, Inc.
of Rutland, Vermont & Tokyo, Japan
with editorial offices at
2-6 Suido 1-chome, Bunkyo-ku, Tokyo 112

© 1992 by Charles E. Tuttle Publishing Co., Inc.

LCC Card No. 92-61823
ISBN 0-8048-1895-9

First edition, 1992

Printed in Japan

CONTENTS

INTRODUCTION

Early in the year 1854 the last vestiges of Japan's almost two-and-a-half centuries of isolationism were swept away when a treaty of trade and friendship was imposed on the nation by Commodore Matthew C. Perry of the United States Navy. In the ensuing twenty years, Japan was to take the first steps toward democracy and industrialization, and rid itself forever of the caste society imposed by feudalism. The rule of the shoguns was drawing to a rapid close.

There can be little doubt that the military power and physical vigor of the Americans came as a surprise and shock to Japan's rulers, whose previous encounters with Westerners had been mainly through a handful of Dutch traders allowed only to exist in a closed and closely guarded encampment near Nagasaki, and Catholic missionaries who had been finally banned from Japan in the 1620s. The American sailors, however, made it totally clear that they were in Japan not simply at the sufferance of the shoguns, and not even as equals, but as the leaders of a new world trading order. The Japanese leaders, to say the least, felt belittled, but what could they do to restore their national pride and show the arrogant barbarians that they were at least equal?

Immediately after the conclusion of the treaty an exchange of gifts was carried out. Toward the conclusion of this ceremony, the Japanese officials informed Commodore Perry that they still had one further gift, and led the Americans ashore to an enclosure surrounded by hundreds of giant sacks of rice. The Americans waited silently, wondering what would happen next. Shortly, twenty-five *rikishi* (sumo wrestlers) stamped down to the sacks and, as a demonstration of their immense strength, picked them up as if they were full of feathers and, to the

Americans' amazement, carried them nonchalantly to the ships for loading.

After this exhibition of brute strength, the Japanese invited the astounded Americans back to the Treaty House, where they set a precedent by becoming the first large group of foreigners to form the audience at a demonstration of sumo. It cannot be said that the Americans were totally overawed by the sight, since contemporary records describe the rikishi as like elephants "in all the bloated fullness of fat and breadth of muscle." The shogunate, however, had succeeded in demonstrating that there were, indeed, Japanese with physical powers way beyond the norm, and this undoubtedly went a little way toward restoring national pride.

Even today in Japan's highly industrialized and modern society, sumo is generally perceived as a quintessentially Japanese sport, in which history, tradition, and even religion are intermingled to form a unique sport of pageantry and splendor perhaps matched by no other country's national sport.

The history of sumo is long and integrally linked with Japan's myths and mores. One legend even relates how around three thousand years ago the ownership of the Japanese islands was decided in a sumo bout between the two gods Takemikazuchi and Takeminakata. After his victory, Takemikazuchi ceded the islands to the Japanese people in perpetuity, and went on to personally establish the imperial line that has remained unbroken right down to today's Emperor Akihito. Few sports can claim such a heritage.

Over the centuries the popularity of sumo has risen and fallen many times, and the sport has evolved from being a religious rite and an entertainment for members of the imperial court, into a genuinely

Detail from a 19th-century woodblock print by Ichiyosai Toyokuni.

popular sport. Rituals and rites have remained virtually unchanged, but nowadays nobody attending one of the six *basho* (tournaments) each year could mistake the screams of the young, female members of the audience as emanating from religious or cultural fervor. Today, rikishi are regarded in the same way as other sportsmen and are often described as handsome, sexy, and even cute.

Even so, the foreign sumo aficionado can hardly fail to notice a modicum of xenophobia among Japanese fans. The relatively recent entry of a significant number of foreigners into sumo was initially regarded by the purists as interesting and even amusing. After all, thought some Japanese, sumo is a sport peculiar to the Japanese psyche, and foreigners, no matter how physically strong, will never be able to cultivate the mental and cultural powers necessary to become *ozeki* (champion) or *yokozuna* (grand champion). How wrong they were.

Foreigners are not actually new to sumo. As far back as the Taisho Era (1912 to 1926), a number of Korean rikishi were active, but since they were citizens of the Japanese empire, they were not regarded as foreigners, merely Japanese once removed. There were even

Japanese-American fighters before the war, with Harley Kiichiro Ozaki of Colorado (fighting under the name Toyonishiki) being the most successful. However, even though he reached the *sekitori* (salaried rikishi) level, Ozaki was not regarded as a genuine foreigner. In fact, trapped in Japan at the outbreak of war, Ozaki was persuaded to take out Japanese citizenship, which he retained until he regained his American nationality in the 1960s. He never returned to the *dohyo* (ring) after the war, since he could barely make enough money to support a wife, and realized that there were less demanding ways of making a living. Instead, he first worked as an interpreter and now, in his early 70s, runs a *ryokan* (Japanese inn) in Tokyo.

The arrival of the first truly foreign, in other words non-Asian, rikishi, and the beginning of what is now often regarded as the Hawaiian challenge, is as recent as February 1964. Jesse James Walani Kuhaulua, later to fight under the name Takamiyama, made his debut in March of the same year in *mae-zumo* (pre-sumo, not listed in the official rankings). The times were about to record major change, but few Japanese sumo fans realized just how much.

TAKAMIYAMA
THE PATHFINDER ARRIVES

On the anniversary of George Washington's birthday, February 22, 1964, nineteen-year-old Jesse James Walani Kuhaulua stepped warily off a plane at Tokyo's Haneda airport into a gray, cold day, unlike anything he had experienced in his first eighteen years of life on the Hawaiian island of Maui. He had come to Japan to join Takasago Beya (Takasago stable), and already felt lonely. He soon discovered that it wasn't only the weather that was depressing. Being expected to sleep in a single, large room with fifty or so other hopefuls, having to rise at four o'clock every morning to train, being fed only twice a day on *chanko-nabe,* a traditional, high-calorie stew (the regular meal of rikishi), and being at the constant beck and call of higher-ranked rikishi, all conspired to make the young Hawaiian doubt he'd made the right choice.

Jesse's entrance to sumo can only be described as an accident, or perhaps it would be better to say, the result of an accident. Years before, while in second grade, Jesse was late for school. Running across a road without really looking where he was going, he was smashed by a truck and flung over twenty yards through the air. Both his legs were damaged and he spent the next six months in hospital recuperating. Even this, however, did not give him a totally clean bill of health. After leaving hospital he discovered that the damage to his legs had resulted in an apparently permanent inability to run fast or long without pain.

Despite his damaged legs, when Jesse entered Baldwin High School, the football coach, Larry Shishido, took one look at his strapping six-feet-two-inches and 280 pounds and informed him he was to become a member of the school football team whether he liked it or not. When Jesse explained to the coach about his weak legs, the sumo world, though

it didn't yet know it, was changed forever. Shishido believed that the practice of sumo was an excellent method of strengthening the legs, and introduced Jesse to the Maui Sumo Club. In a very short time the strapping Hawaiian was a local success.

Jesse trained with the club for several years, but never thought or dreamed of training and competing with the professionals in Japan. In fact, his ambition at the time was to join Hawaii's finest and become a policeman. What this would have done to counter Hawaii's growing crime figures we will never know.

Hawaii's criminals, however, got a break when a group of Japan's top sekitori, including Taiho and Kashiwado, leading yokozuna, and led by *oyakata* (sumo stablemaster) Takasago visited the islands for an exhibition tournament. After a day of training during which Jesse and his fellow club members went up against the top professionals and, in his own words, were "tossed around like so many paper sacks filled with feathers," he returned tired and bruised to the locker room. A lifetime in the police force seemed a step nearer.

Soon afterwards, however, he was told that Takasago wanted to meet him, and, much to his astonishment, was offered a place in Takasago Beya. Despite Jesse's eagerness, not everybody in his family was happy with the offer. It took quite some time to convince his mother to let him go, but finally he boarded the plane, landed in Tokyo, and in a matter of a few years changed the face of sumo.

Jesse, or Takamiyama as he became known, made excellent progress after his debut in March 1964, when he weighed a svelte (for him) 253 pounds. Over the years his weight increased to almost twice that. In May that year he captured the *yusho* (championship)

The Facts: TAKAMIYAMA (AZUMAZEKI)

NAME: Jesse Kuhaulua
BORN: June 16, 1944, Maui, Hawaii
HIGHEST RANK: Sekiwake
HEIGHT: 6' 3½"
FIGHTING WEIGHT: 452 lbs.
ENTERED MAKUNOUCHI: January, 1968
STABLE (WHEN FIGHTING): Takasago

in the lowest *jonokuchi* division. This was followed two months later by a win in the next highest division, *jonidan*. Three years after his debut, in March 1967, he was promoted to *juryo* (the second-highest division) as the first ever non-Asian rikishi. Early in 1968, he made it into the top *makunouchi* division, where he remained for the next sixteen years. The highest rank Takamiyama ever reached was *sekiwake*, the third-highest rank in sumo, and his most glorious day was undoubtedly when he became the first non-Japanese to win a basho, at Nagoya in July 1972.

Over the years, Takamiyama became immensely popular as a rikishi and even gained fame as a television personality. It was assumed by most that when he retired from the ring, he would become a sumo *toshiyori* (elder). However, in 1976, the Sumo Association announced that only rikishi of Japanese nationality would be allowed to stay in the sumo world after retirement. The reasons were never explained, but some commentators believe it was a move to stop retired foreigners from becoming dominant in the sport, as they had in most of Japan's other martial arts.

Takamiyama really had no choice if he wanted to stay in the only profession he had known, and in June 1980 he took Japanese citizenship and a new Japanese name, Daigoro Watanabe, Watanabe being his wife's maiden name. Upon his retirement from the dohyo, he was given yet another sumo name, and became Azumazeki Oyakata.

In April 1986, Takamiyama yet again broke new ground when he became the first non-Asian rikishi to open his own stable, Azumazeki Beya, initially training Japanese rikishi, but then taking on several foreigners, including another Hawaiian, Chad Rowan, now fighting for sumo supremacy and promotion to yokozuna under the name Akebono.

(p. 10) Takamiyama, the biggest man, and one of the biggest draws, in sumo in 1978.

LEFT: Takamiyama enters the dohyo in his last ceremonial kesho-mawashi (apron) in 1984. Each apron costs between $7,500 and $35,000.

BELOW: Takamiyama performs the pre-match ritual in 1981. The ritual quite often lasts much longer than the actual match.

ABOVE LEFT: An introspective Takamiyama before a fight in 1978.

ABOVE: A force to be reckoned with, Takamiyama in his prime.

LEFT: Takamiyama prepares for battle at a hanazumo (exhibition tournament) in 1978.

RIGHT: Takamiyama's sheer size made it difficult for smaller rikishi to get to the belt.

LEFT: Man-mountain Takamiyama takes on ozeki Takanohana, the father of the Waka-Taka brothers, in 1978.

BELOW: Takamiyama (*fourth from left*) participates in the opening ceremony of the July 1982 basho.

RIGHT: Takamiyama cuts the topknot of former sekiwake Kurohimeyama at his danpatsu-shiki (retirement ceremony) in 1982. Both rikishi entered sumo in March 1964.

BELOW: Takamiyama's stablemaster Takasago Oyakata (former yokozuna Asashio) makes the final cut to the rikishi's topknot at his danpatsu-shiki in February 1985.

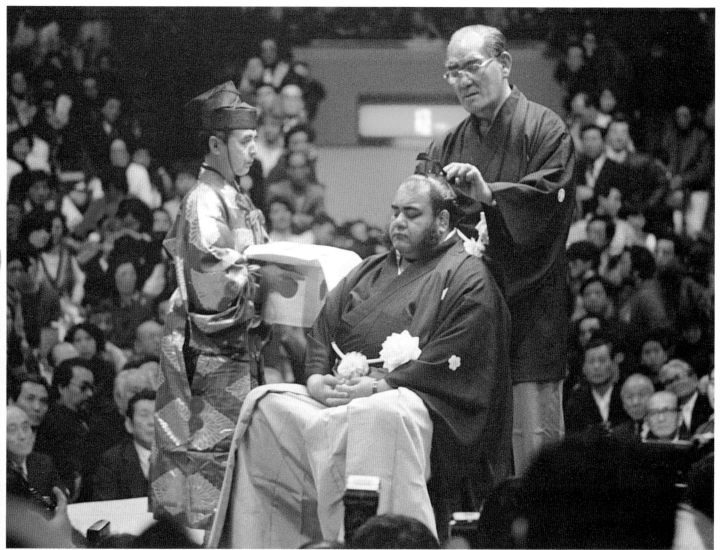

AZUMAZEKI OYAKATA
TRAINING THE FORCES

In February 1985, then American Ambassador to Japan Mike Mansfield attended Jesse's *danpatsu-shiki* (official retirement ceremony) at a packed Ryogoku Kokugikan (Tokyo's sumo stadium), along with 11,000 other fans and well-wishers. During the four-hour ceremony, Jesse charmed everyone with his patented mixture of Japanese respectful behavior and openly friendly Hawaiian bonhomie. He spent a couple of hours bearhugging anyone who came in sight, kissing babies, and backslapping those he couldn't or wouldn't kiss or bearhug, as well as posing for a seemingly endless number of photographs. Said Ambassador Mansfield, "As a former politician, I am thankful I never had to come up against an opponent like Takamiyama."

After opening his own stable in 1986, Azumazeki Oyakata, as he is now known, soon attracted several foreigners, including fellow Hawaiian Akebono, but to this day he is insistent that he runs a traditional stable, not something specifically designed for the accommodation of foreigners. He treats the foreigners no differently from the Japanese.

A typical day for a young sumo trainee begins around four-thirty each morning. By five o'clock he is in the *keikoba* (training area), doing his warming up exercises. Next he enters the ring and competes with other trainees in a series of elimination contests, where the winner of each bout stays in the ring until he is finally beaten. This contest is followed by a series of bouts with the same opponent. Finally there is an exercise where one wrestler, the attacker, continuously tries to push another fighter, the defender, out of the ring. From warming up to the end of training is usually about two hours. Then the work really begins.

About seven o'clock, some trainees stay in the keikoba as *tsukebito* (servant, apprentice) to the sekitori, and carry out such menial duties as wiping the senior rikishi's sweaty brows and bodies or fetching drinks. Other trainees go on *chankoban* (kitchen duty) and have to prepare the first meal of the day.

At about eleven o'clock the senior rikishi and the stablemaster take their baths, attended throughout by trainees. Immediately after bathing, the seniors sit down to their meal of chanko-nabe, served by the same tsukebito who prepared it. The trainees on waiter service have to be extremely careful, for even a minor infraction of the rules such as leaving a plate empty until a senior rikishi has to ask for more, can result in severe physical chastisement.

When the seniors have finished eating, the tsukebito are allowed to eat the leftovers before finally getting a chance to bathe themselves. After bathing, the tsukebito are either back on kitchen duty, washing pots and pans, or act as housemaids by cleaning the higher-ranked rikishi's rooms, airing the bedding, and carrying out many other menial tasks. By the time these chores are finished, it is time to prepare the second meal of the day, which usually begins around six o'clock in the evening, and for which the same hierarchical rules as in the morning prevail. When the meal is finished, the trainees clear up yet again before finally being allowed to drag themselves off to bed at around nine o'clock. The same routine starts again at four-thirty the next morning.

The fact that Azumazeki survived this harsh regime, and is now in a position to guide others through the cultural and dietary minefields, brought hope to younger foreigners, including Salevaa Atisanoe, Konishiki, who now fights as ozeki.

LEFT: Several years after retirement from the dohyo, Takamiyama was made a tournament shinpan (judge). This photograph was taken in 1992.

BELOW: Azumazeki celebrates fellow Hawaiian Akebono's first yusho in May 1992. On the right, Azumazeki's wife pours sake.

AZUMAZEKI OYAKATA

KONISHIKI
THE GIANT THREAT

In 1986 the Japanese rikishi Kitao, who had had a reasonable record for several tournaments, but who had never won the yusho, was promoted to yokozuna and given the new name Futahaguro. Over the next year and five months he still failed to win a tournament, beat up several of the tsukebito at his stable, and eventually was forced to resign after rudely pushing aside the wife of his stablemaster. This was exactly the opposite of the image the Sumo Association wanted to present and certain changes were suggested to vet future yokozuna aspirants.

In March 1992, immediately after Salevaa Atisanoe (Konishiki), the Samoan-Hawaiian, won his third tournament, Sadogatake (former yokozuna Kotozakura), a director of the Sumo Association's judging department, said, "Winning a tournament is a big factor, but his promotion may be discussed after the next tourney. The way he lost two matches did not look good." Unlike Futahaguro, Konishiki certainly wasn't going to be the blue-eyed, or perhaps in this case brown-eyed, baby of the Sumo Association and receive early promotion. In fact, it now seems that in order to be promoted from ozeki, sumo's second-highest rank, to yokozuna, the former Honolulu football player will have to win two tournaments back-to-back, an extremely difficult feat. But Konishiki shows no signs of giving up.

Still only 28 years old when the above statement was made, Konishiki's commitment to sumo and Japan is unquestionable. He once said that he liked the simplicity of the sport, "If you win you go up; if you lose you go down." And since his entry into sumo he has almost always been on the winning side each tournament, getting at least eight wins out of the fifteen bouts and receiving promotion. It is only for that final

step up the ladder to yokozuna that stricter rules are enforced, and probably rightly so, since a yokozuna can never be demoted. If he loses embarrassingly, he can't go down, he has to retire.

Even so, there is suspicion in some circles that Konishiki's bid for promotion is being stalled primarily because of his nationality. In fact *Nihon Keizai Shimbun*, a leading financial and business daily, rather dubiously quoted Konishiki in April 1992 as saying that he had not been promoted to yokozuna for reasons of racism. However, at a press conference a few days after the article was published, Konishiki absolutely denied having made this remark and with what seems unbeatable logic explained, "I don't even know the damn word for racism."

He may not have actually accused the sumo world of racism in so many words, but could there be any truth in the charges? In a magazine article published just after Konishiki's alleged statement, Noboru Kojima, a member of the Sumo Association advisory committee that considers promotions to yokozuna rank, said, "Foreign yokozuna are not needed." Another insider of the Sumo Association told the English-language *Mainichi Daily News*, "Speaking frankly, I would say that our true feelings are that we wouldn't like to see a foreign rikishi become a yokozuna, because we don't want to see Japanese wrestlers walking behind foreign wrestlers. We don't show this opinion to outsiders, but just as before there is a strong anti-Konishiki faction."

There is, however, also a strong pro-Konishiki sentiment among many Japanese fans. He remains extremely popular, has married a beautiful Japanese fashion model, and expects soon to take out Japanese nationality. These factors may have taken some of the

The Facts: *KONISHIKI*

NAME: Salevaa Atisanoe
BORN: December 31, 1963, Oahu, Hawaii
HIGHEST RANK: Ozeki*
HEIGHT: 6' 1½"
WEIGHT: 582 lbs.*
ENTERED MAKUNOUCHI: July, 1984
STABLE: Takasago
* as of October, 1992

sting out of the sight of Japanese rikishi being regularly squashed by the Hawaiian behemoth, who at his fighting heaviest weighed in at over 580 pounds.

Konishiki's personality may also be a significant factor in his popularity, being extremely intelligent and cultured, unlike many professional sportsmen. Before he was spotted by Takamiyama he was near the top of his class at University High School in Honolulu and intended to go on to college and study for a law degree. He may never have become the Hawaiian Perry Mason, but if Takamiyama had missed him, sumo would have lost a truly great rikishi and personality.

Though massive, even by sumo standards, and aggressive when fighting, Konishiki has a remarkably soft voice and gentle manners. He seems to combine at least two different characters. At morning practice, for example, he will regularly chastise the trainees by smacking them with a bamboo stick in order to make

them reach the level of rage he believes they need to become better rikishi. Once practice is over, however, his time is spent studying Japanese, in which he is almost fluent, taking classical piano lessons on a weekly basis, wining and dining with sponsors, and, probably less so now that he is married, going to discos. He once said, "I can't run for hours, but I can dance for hours."

It is to be hoped that Konishiki dances his way through many more tournaments to the enjoyment of his millions of fans and to the terror of his opponents. Though he may not make that last step to sumo's top rank, through simply not being consistently good enough, he has gone a stage further than Takamiyama. He has also proved that foreigners have got what it takes to make it to the highest levels, and has set a precedent that other Hawaiian rikishi, such as Akebono and Fiamal Penitani (Musashimaru), may very well be able to build on.

(p. 20) Konishiki receives sumo's most prestigious prize, the Emperor's Cup, after winning the 1992 Haru basho in Osaka.

LEFT: Konishiki enters the dohyo in January 1991. The character on his kesho-mawashi reads "Katsu," meaning "Victory."

BELOW: Konishiki, by far the biggest man currently in sumo, faces off against Toyonoumi.

Konishiki fights for the belt and control of center ring with Misugisato.

ABOVE LEFT: A yobidashi announces the next bout as Konishiki waits to enter the dohyo.

ABOVE RIGHT: Konishiki's sheer size can intimidate some opponents.

BELOW: The Hawaiians clash, with Konishiki facing off against Akebono.

LEFT: Konishiki bulldozes Misugisato out of the dohyo.

ABOVE: Toyonoumi tries to get in below Konishiki to maneuver him out.

BELOW LEFT: Konishiki takes the winner's envelope on the last day of the 1989 Nagoya basho.

BELOW: Konishiki heads down to the dohyo amid awed fans.

ABOVE LEFT: The kyokai goaisatsu in May 1992. Konishiki is second from left, Akebono is second from right, and Musashimaru is behind the speaker.

ABOVE: Konishiki participates in former komusubi Maenoshiri's danpatsu-shiki in October 1990.

LEFT: Konishiki enters the ring at the 1992 Nagoya basho in his favorite America-Japan kesho-mawashi.

BELOW: Konishiki at morning training at Takasago Beya in 1991.

ABOVE: Konishiki jokes with Nankairyu, a Samoan who made it to maegashira, but then dropped out.

RIGHT: Konishiki fools around while preparing for a jungyo.

BELOW: Konishiki (right) and Musashimaru (center) at the shitaku-beya in Tokyo's Kokugikan.

BELOW RIGHT: Konishiki in an expansive mood.

AKEBONO
VYING FOR SUPREMACY

Konishiki, in his rapid climb through the ranks, made it to ozeki in the fastest time ever, taking just thirty basho to reach the top-but-one spot in 1987. In May 1992, however, this record wasn't just beaten, it was destroyed. Fellow Hawaiian Chad Haheo Rowan, fighting as Akebono, was promoted to ozeki after a mere twenty-six basho. What made it an even greater moment for the Hawaiians was that Konishiki had been discovered by Takamiyama, now stablemaster Azumazeki, for his former Takasago Beya, and Akebono had been recruited by Azumazeki after he started his own stable.

To say that the six-foot-eight-inch former high school basketball player's astronomic success came as a surprise to his stablemaster would be something of an understatement. Said Azumazeki, "It's like a dream. I didn't think I could have an ozeki this soon." When asked what plans he had for the fighter after he had clinched the tournament championship, leading to his promotion, Azumazeki sardonically replied, "More practice."

That practice could be the key to Akebono becoming the first non-Asian yokozuna. No doubt the classes in grappling he now takes day after day are considerably different from those he attended at Hawaii's Pacific University, but the aim of achieving improvement has to be the same. And it seems that despite his height and high center of gravity, often considered negative attributes for a rikishi, Akebono has a positive attitude toward the practice and perfection of his skills.

Said Azumazeki in an interview with *Kyodo News Service,* "When I [first] saw his practice I was disappointed because he looked very shaky, as he has a high center of gravity. To tell the truth, I was more

interested in his younger brother [who tried sumo but dropped out] because he has a much more suitable physique for being a rikishi. But Akebono turned out to be a quick learner. When I taught him a certain technique, he not only consumed what I taught but also remodeled it. I was even a little worried about it because slow and steady is the name of the game in sumo."

After Akebono's tournament championship, however, various members of the Japanese and foreign press didn't appear to think that slow and steady was a reasonable description of the growing dominance of Hawaiians in Japan's most traditional sport. After all, this was the second tournament in a row to be won by a Hawaiian. Even the American government, forgetting Japan's unwillingness to import rice for a few moments, got in on the act, with American Ambassador Michael Armacost entering the dohyo to read a letter of congratulation from President George Bush, in continuation of a gesture started when Takamiyama won his yusho back in 1972.

Despite the presidential congratulations, Akebono has not let the fame and glory go to his head. In fact he seems to be intent on simply becoming an outstanding rikishi by following the rules to the letter, saying in an interview with the English-language *The Daily Yomiuri,* "It [following the rules] is something you have to do. You cannot become a good sumo wrestler and not live the lifestyle. I guess you have to learn the lifestyle first. That is how you become a good sumo wrestler . . . . He [Konishiki] has been here ten or eleven years. Me, I'm still learning. The Japanese have been living this life ever since they were a baby. You can compare me with a four-year-old Japanese baby. So when you ask me if I've got plans for the future, all

The Facts: AKEBONO

NAME: Chadwick Rowan
BORN: May 8, 1969, Oahu, Hawaii
HIGHEST RANK: Ozeki*
HEIGHT: 6' 8¼"
WEIGHT: 454 lbs.*
ENTERED MAKUNOUCHI: September, 1990
STABLE: Azumazeki
* as of October, 1992

I know right now is next week, next month. That is all I worry about. Right now, I just go to practice."

Practice he says and, no doubt, practice he does. But his rise to ozeki rank has also brought him certain privileges and a slightly easier lifestyle. He likes to spend his free time watching movies and listening to music, telling a reporter from *The Japan Times,* "When it's tournament time I like to watch stuff like *Rocky,* to get powered up for the tournament. Then in off times I watch sad movies, love stories. The same goes for music . . . When it's time to get pumped up I listen to rock and stuff like that; when it's time to relax I listen to classical music."

He may be a fan of classical music, but some purist Japanese sumo fans claim that Akebono, along with the other earlier Hawaiians, relies too much on non-classical sumo techniques and his mind-boggling size and strength, and has failed to master the more technically demanding arm and leg throws. This, they claim, is among the main reasons why neither Konishiki nor Akebono should ever be made yokozuna. Whether this is a valid criticism or not, the doubt remains as to if there will ever be a Hawaiian technically capable of satisfying the purists in a way that Konishiki and even Akebono have yet failed to do. A very few Japanese are answering yes to this question and pointing at yet another up-and-coming Hawaiian rikishi, Fiamal Penitani, who fights under the name Musashimaru. It seems that whatever happens, the Hawaiian tide continues to flow.

(p. 30) Akebono receives the Emperor's Cup after winning the May 1992 basho.

LEFT: Akebono enters the arena on his way to the dohyo in a traditional kesho-mawashi in 1991.

BELOW: Akebono gets into the right mood before a fight.

Akebono defeats Wakahanada
on the final day of the May 1992
basho, thereby winning his first
yusho.

ABOVE: Niramiai: He who stares, wins. Takatoriki and Akebono.

RIGHT: The throwing of salt is part of the cleansing ritual before each bout.

BELOW: Akebono prepares for the initial thrust.

AKEBONO

ABOVE: Getting a hold on the belt can be vitally important.
RIGHT: Akebono stuns Wakahanada.
BELOW: Akebono deals Wakahanada a crushing blow.

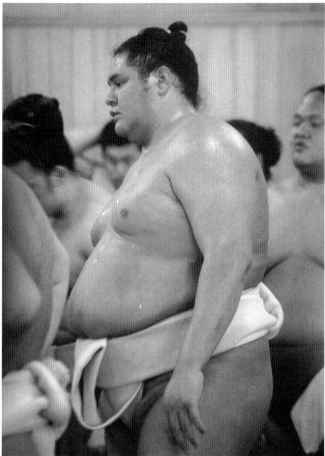

ABOVE: Akebono in front of Azumazeki Beya. The calligraphy on the sign was written by former Prime Minister Yasuhiro Nakasone.

ABOVE RIGHT: Akebono preparing for training at Azumazeki Beya.

RIGHT: The new man on the dohyo. Akebono in his juryo days, April 1990.

AKEBONO

RIGHT: Akebono raises a smile as he enters Tokyo's Kokugikan.

BELOW and BELOW RIGHT: Chankonabe, the traditional food of rikishi, can contain many ingredients. Foreign rikishi often have trouble getting used to it.

5

MUSASHIMARU
THE PEOPLE'S CHOICE

Just prior to the Nagoya basho, in July 1992, Konishiki stood six-foot-one-and-a-half inches and tipped the scales at 582 pounds, the heaviest man in sumo. Akebono, his Hawaiian rival, though having had to pull out of the tournament because of injury, weighed in at 445 pounds and stood six-foot-eight-and-a-quarter inches tall, the tallest man in sumo. Fiamal Penitani, Musashimaru, only the fourth Hawaiian ever to reach the *sanyaku* ranks (the top four ranks in sumo), measured six-foot-three-and-a-quarter inches and weighed in at 395 pounds, neither the tallest nor the heaviest fighter, but certainly one of the most watched by Japanese and foreign fans alike.

For twenty-eight years, ever since the arrival on the dohyo of the first Hawaiian, Takamiyama, Japanese sumo fans had watched, sometimes with awe, the inroads made into the land's traditional sport by the foreigners. Takamiyama made it to sekiwake, sumo's third-highest rank, and both Konishiki and Akebono went a step further to ozeki, the sport's second-highest rank. At the Nagoya basho, twenty-one-year-old Musashimaru was ranked *komusubi* (junior champion second class), sumo's fourth-highest position.

During the 1992 Nagoya basho sumo fans discussed Konishiki's dismal record in his previous outing and agonized over his potential to ace the latest tournament and get another shot at promotion to yokozuna. He didn't. In fact, he demonstrated a worrying inconsistency and didn't seem able to win either the big matches or cope with his smaller, more agile opponents. Fans were also disappointed with Akebono, who, having just been promoted to ozeki at the end of the previous basho, had had to withdraw because of an injury suffered during practice. Eyes, therefore, were on Musashimaru, and he didn't disappoint, finishing

with an eleven–four record for the fifteen matches in the two-week tournament and earning the Technique award.

Musashimaru's rise to komusubi rank was the second-fastest in sumo history, having taken him only seventeen tournaments. The record for the fastest is still held by Konishiki, who took only fifteen. But perhaps more important is where Musashimaru will go from here. Currently he is successfully emerging from the long shadows cast by the two Hawaiian ozeki, but it may only be a matter of time before he emerges as the Hawaiian most likely to succeed in sumo. In fact, two weeks prior to the September 1992 basho in Tokyo, Musashimaru was promoted to sekiwake, sumo's third-highest rank. This made him equal to Takamiyama's highest-ever rank, and only one step behind both Konishiki and Akebono.

Several factors could influence Musashimaru's progress. First, he is not as tall as Akebono. Though certainly no midget, at least nine of the Japanese in the top division are taller than him. Second, he is nowhere near as heavy as Konishiki. At least six current Japanese rikishi are heavier. Third, his body-weight-to-height ratio gives him a much lower center of gravity, a definite advantage in sumo. Finally, he doesn't rely as heavily as Konishiki and Akebono on slapping and thrusting attacks, but instead is developing a more comprehensive array of traditional sumo fighting techniques.

At twenty-one, Musashimaru has a two-year-age advantage on Akebono and can give Konishiki seven-and-a-half years, though at the time of the September 1992 basho he was only one rank behind. He also seems to be quickly catching up with the two Hawaiian front-runners in the popularity stakes. Perhaps be-

The Facts: **MUSASHIMARU**

NAME: Fiamal Penitani
BORN: May 2, 1971, Oahu, Hawaii
HIGHEST RANK: Sekiwake*
HEIGHT: 6' 3¼"
WEIGHT: 383 lbs.*
ENTERED MAKUNOUCHI: November, 1991
STABLE: Musashigawa
* as of October, 1992

cause he is physically more of the norm for rikishi, or even because some fans claim that he looks like Saigo Takamori, a rebel of the 1870s with a Robin Hood-like level of popularity, Japanese sumo fans feel more comfortable with Musashimaru than with the other Hawaiians.

Another reason for his burgeoning popularity could well be that he doesn't belong to either one of the stables with popular rikishi, or a stable with other foreigners. In fact, he is the first rikishi from the Musashigawa Beya, run by former yokozuna Mienoumi, to reach the sanyaku ranks. His stablemaster seems relatively satisfied with his progress, but is constantly pushing him to improve his basic techniques. Also, Musashimaru, unlike the other foreigners, doesn't seem to have any trouble adjusting to the various training methods used traditionally to strengthen the lower parts of the body, so necessary to successfully maneuver struggling, slapping, and squirming behemoths across a ring and out.

Many Japanese sumo fans seem to have taken Musashimaru to their hearts and are expecting great things of him. Almost everyone admits that both Konishiki and Akebono are masters of force, but many claim that the other two Hawaiians do not have the technical skills necessary in the long term to continually beat the next generation of up-and-coming Japanese rikishi led by Wakahanada and Takahanada, known affectionately as the Waka-Taka brothers, currently the most popular duo in the sumo world. Indeed, there is a growing belief in sumo circles that the next Japanese yokozuna could well be Takahanada, son of former ozeki Takanohana and nephew of former yokozuna Wakanohana. Musashimaru is likewise favored by many as the most likely foreign contender. If he achieves it, he would be the first foreigner to reach such an exalted rank. The battle is definitely on and the sumo world breathlessly awaits the outcome of future battles between the three Hawaiian titans and the popular Waka-Taka brothers.

(p. 40) Musashimaru accepts one of the sansho prizes after the September 1991 basho in Tokyo.

LEFT: The "maru" in Musashimaru's name means ship, hence the nautical kesho-mawashi.

BELOW: A pensive Musashimaru preparing for battle.

No longer pensive, Musashi-maru takes on Takatoriki.

ABOVE: Musashimaru psyches himself up before a bout with Wakahanada.

LEFT: The battle commences between Musashimaru and Wakahanada.

BELOW: Musashimaru neatly disposes of Takatoriki.

ABOVE: Terao gets on the wrong side of Musashimaru.

LEFT: Musashimaru collects the winner's envelope.

BELOW: Musashimaru (left), Kirishima, and Akinoshima take part in the ceremonial opening.

MUSASHIMARU

ABOVE LEFT: Fame at last. Musashimaru is interviewed for Japanese television after a winning bout.

ABOVE RIGHT: Musashimaru relaxes in the shitaku-beya before a bout.

BELOW LEFT: Musashimaru relaxes with Takeru while on tour.

BELOW RIGHT: Musashimaru entering the gymnasium in Nagoya after his promotion to juryo in July 1991.

THE WAKA-TAKA BROTHERS
THE RESISTANCE REGROUPS

On the first day of the May 1991 sumo tournament, the man known to his millions of fans as The Wolf, thirty-five-year-old yokozuna Chiyonofuji, the winner of thirty-one tournaments and 1,044 individual matches, faced a boy just half his age, the number-one *maegashira* (a member of the top division, but below the sanyaku ranks), Takahanada. Taka came in low, causing the yokozuna to resort to every trick in the book to shake him off, but without success. Takahanada drove the yokozuna back steadily before eventually bulldozing him out of the dohyo. The aging Chiyonofuji read the writing on the wall and retired two days later after a further humiliating loss.

Many Japanese sumo enthusiasts saw this as the changing of the generations, as had happened thirteen years before when the twenty-two-year-old Chiyonofuji beat aging ozeki Takanohana, Takahanada's father, thereby hastening his retirement. Takanohana had been one of the most popular rikishi of the 1970s. Though never quite making it to yokozuna because of his light, but muscular physique, his boyish good looks and mastery of technique made him extremely popular with sumo fanatics and young women alike. After retirement from the dohyo Takanohana took the name Fujishima and started his own *heya* (stable), eventually taking on as trainees his two sons, now fighting under the names Wakahanada and Takahanada.

Both sons joined the heya, moving from the private family quarters to the communal trainees' dormitory, in their teens. Initially, Wakahanada, the older brother, did better, moving quite rapidly up the ranks, but very soon the younger brother's superior sumo physique began to develop quickly and Takahanada began to gain the ascendancy.

Wakahanada, at five-foot-nine inches, has not yet developed the muscular frame of his six-foot-one-inch younger brother, but is still seen by many as an eventual contender for ozeki, the sport's second-highest rank, due to his comprehensive arsenal of techniques.

Takahanada, on the other hand, has not only developed a muscular physique capable on his good days of cowing all but the strongest rikishi, but has honed his baby-face good looks and self-deprecating charm to such a pitch that very few Japanese females, be they teenagers, homemakers, or grandmothers, can watch him without a definite trembling of the knees. On the day that he beat Chiyonofuji, for example, 44.4 percent of Japan's total television audience tuned in to watch and dream.

But Takahanada is not just a pretty face. Among the many firsts he has collected in his brief career are: youngest rikishi ever to beat a yokozuna; youngest to reach the sanyaku ranks; youngest to win the Fighting Spirit award; youngest to win the Technique award; youngest to win the Outstanding Performance award; and, probably to cap it all, in January 1992 he became the youngest rikishi ever to win a tournament.

The tournament win turned out to be a real family affair. Stablemaster and father, Fujishima, admitted that there was nothing more he could teach him at the present, and the *Tennoshihai* (The Emperor's Cup), the most prestigious prize in sumo, was presented by the head of the Sumo Association, Futagoyama, Takahanada's uncle, former yokozuna Wakanohana. The only slightly ironic spot in the entire proceedings was when, as a nineteen year old, Takahanada was not allowed the celebratory drink of *sake* (rice wine) from the giant cup. The legal drinking age in Japan is

The Facts: WAKAHANADA (far left)
NAME: Masaru Hanada
BORN: January 20, 1971, Tokyo
HIGHEST RANK: Komusubi*
HEIGHT: 5' 9"   WEIGHT: 278 lbs.*
ENTERED MAKUNOUCHI: September, 1990
STABLE: Fujishima

The Facts: TAKAHANADA (left)
NAME: Koji Hanada
BORN: August 12, 1972, Tokyo
HIGHEST RANK: Sekiwake*
HEIGHT: 6' 1"   WEIGHT: 287 lbs.*
ENTERED MAKUNOUCHI: May, 1990
STABLE: Fujishima
* as of October, 1992

twenty, no matter how famous or popular you may be, and the police had made it very clear that they expected the law to be obeyed.

Even so, it was obvious that a new and home-grown hero was emerging. Here at last, said the sumo buffs, was a Japanese rikishi capable of turning back the waves of the Hawaiian tide. The women, however, seemed more interested in the man than the moment. In the English-language *Mainichi Daily News* Yuji Fukuda, an executive at Dentsu, Inc., the world's largest advertising company, explained, "The nation has lacked heros in general, and everybody has been looking for one. His [Takahanada's] physical strength combined with his image as a naive little brother, instead of a macho man, is very appealing to young women." In fact, shortly after his win, Takahanada became only the second ever male to appear on the front cover of the very popular teenage girl's magazine *an an*.

But real achievements in sumo cannot be measured solely by the number of swooning teenage fans. Winning is what matters. Although he has not yet reached a level considered to be anywhere near invincible, Takahanada did seal Konishiki's ill-fated bid for yokozuna rank in the May 1992 tournament by handing him his fourth defeat of the basho, making the Hawaiian look really bad. This was seen by some as Japan's first resurgent step.

Now that the Japanese have their popular champions, Takahanada and his slightly less powerful and sexy brother Wakahanada, the scene is set for one of the most exciting periods of sumo history. Can the handsome, charming, traditionally brought up, technically brilliant Waka-Taka brothers take the sport by storm and inherit their father's and uncle's mantles as the princes of sumo? Or will the power and individualism of the Americans, Konishiki, Akebono, and Musashimaru, simply overcome the young Japanese brothers and lead the sumo world into a period of Hawaiian dominance of Japan's most famous sport?

(p. 50) ABOVE: Wakahanada receives an award at an exhibition tournament.
BELOW: Takahanada receives the yusho award in the January 1992 basho.

LEFT: Wakahanada with a traditional Mount Fuji motif kesho-mawashi.

ABOVE: Wakahanada psyches himself up for a bout.

LEFT: Wearing a modern, abstract kesho-mawashi, Takahanada takes part in the opening ceremony .

BELOW: Takahanada carries out the pre-bout ritual.

Wakahanada tries to maneuver Konishiki to the edge in the 1991 Nagoya basho.

Takahanada fends off the smaller, but troublesome Itai in 1990.

LEFT: Wakahanada prepares for the initial charge.
BELOW: Wakahanada (*left*) and Akebono prepare for battle.

BELOW: Wakahanada (*right*) grapples for the belt with Daishoyama.

THE WAKA-TAKA BROTHERS

LEFT: Takahanada, currently the most popular rikishi, tries to outstare his opponent.

ABOVE: Takahanada faces off against yokozuna Chiyonofuji in May 1991. Takahanada's win that day made Chiyonofuji's retirement inevitable.

BELOW: Takahanada fights for control of the dohyo against Kirishima in July 1992.

THE WAKA-TAKA BROTHERS

ABOVE: The big and the beautiful. Konishiki and Takahanada face off in March 1991.

ABOVE RIGHT: The fight for the belt. Konishiki and Takahanada in March 1991.

BELOW: Konishiki resorts to slaps. March 1991.

RIGHT: At the edge. Konishiki tries to belly-out Takahanada. March 1991.

THE WAKA-TAKA BROTHERS

Two other challengers for supremacy. Kirishima *(above)* was the only Japanese ozeki in the September 1992 basho, and Mitoizumi *(right)*, known as The Big Salt, won the yusho in the 1992 Nagoya Basho. But there are many others *(below)* hoping to make it to the top in sumo.

INTERNATIONALIZATION VS. NATIONALISM

The question now facing the leaders of the sumo world is whether or not the sport will become internationalized along the lines of other martial arts such as judo, karate, and kendo. Perhaps more to the point is the question whether they really want it to be internationalized to the extent where Japanese rikishi could be seen walking behind foreigners.

It is, after all, not unheard of for the organizers of a sport to consider it internationalized while at the same time keeping other nationalities from competing. A good example of this could be baseball's World Series, where the world is reduced to teams from North America, and the *world* champion, therefore, is inevitably either American or Canadian. If the Japanese were to follow this example, could other countries really complain?

There are several facts, however, that point to a willingness on the part of the Sumo Association to allow the sport to escape from the confines of isolationism. First, there is the fact that Azumazeki, former rikishi Takamiyama, though Hawaiian born, is now the head of a successful stable. Second, it cannot be denied that two Hawaiians, Konishiki and Akebono, have been promoted to sumo's second-highest rank of ozeki. Third, it should be noted that Musashimaru is quite openly being touted, particularly since his promotion to sekiwake, by many Japanese as likely to be the first foreign yokozuna. Finally, recent years have seen exhibition tournaments being held abroad in such places as Hawaii, London, Barcelona, and Dusseldorf. New plans are now being made for future exhibitions in Hawaii, California, and Hong Kong, as well as a possible return to London and other European cities.

The other side of these coins, however, are as follow. First, Takamiyama had to give up his American citizenship and become Japanese before being allowed to open his heya. This rule still applies and there are no signs that a change is even being considered. As a result, Konishiki has already submitted his naturalization papers, and Akebono and Musashimaru will have to do the same if they want to stay associated with sumo after retirement from the dohyo.

Second, although Konishiki was promoted to ozeki, and has won three tournaments and been runner-up eight times, there seems little hope that he will be promoted to yokozuna. This is even though his nearest Japanese rival, Kirishima (who has won one tournament and been runner-up six times), is thirty-three, the oldest wrestler currently in the top division, and the fifth-oldest in sumo as a whole. Some people are suspicious that the organizers are waiting until a likely Japanese contender comes along before choosing the next yokozuna.

Third, it is true that Musashimaru is the current Hawaiian darling of many Japanese fans, but, at the time of writing, he had not won a tournament, and was not, therefore, seen as an immediate threat. If he were to win the next couple of tournaments, the situation would be extremely interesting.

Finally, although the London, Barcelona, and Dusseldorf exhibitions were undoubted successes, none of the wins recorded by rikishi at these venues count toward their career records. In this way the foreign non-official tournaments are similar to the Battle of the Sexes in tennis between Jimmy Connors and Martina Navratilova. They provide entertainment, but don't count in the ratings.

It is highly unlikely that official tournaments will

LEFT: Sumo fever gripped Britain, as shown by these newspapers during the 1991 exhibition tournament.

ever be held outside Japan, but there is a distinct possibility of an increased number of foreign tours, and even annual exhibition tournaments in foreign cities. If, for example, the Waka-Taka brothers enjoy their trips abroad, they may come to believe in the idea of spreading the pleasure and pageantry of sumo on a global scale. In another thirty years, when the brothers may well be leading the Sumo Association, accompanied it is hoped by Konishiki, Akebono, and Musashimaru, some changes may be made.

Until then, however, sumo fans will almost always have to visit Japan to watch the sport in the six annual basho, at Tokyo (three times a year), Osaka, Nagoya,

and Fukuoka (each once a year). Even so, the next few years will probably be some of the most exciting the ancient sport has ever experienced. The leadership in automobile making may have moved from Detroit to Nagoya, and electronic wizardry may have emigrated from California to Japan, but there is still a distinct possibility that some of the top rikishi, at least for a couple of generations, may come from the spiritual descendants of Kamehama, the Caesar of Hawaii, and who might even lead their followers into a much more widely accepted and considerably more internationalized world of sumo.

Aloha.

(p. 60) London's Royal Albert Hall played host to 1991's largest exhibition tournament.

280-pound Kirishima prepares to take on Konishiki's 582 pounds.

High hopes. Konishiki prepares
to defend himself in London in
1991.

ABOVE: Akebono takes demonstration bouts just as seriously as the real thing.

ABOVE RIGHT: Akebono, just prior to the first leap.

RIGHT: It is not easy for smaller rikishi to get a hold of Konishiki, even in demonstration tournaments.

ABOVE: Konishiki in London. Enough to stop the traffic.

RIGHT: It's not all fighting. Konishiki in festive clothes.

BELOW: Akebono gets the bird in London.

BELOW RIGHT: Wakahanada *(left)* and Wakashoyo take a stroll in a London park.

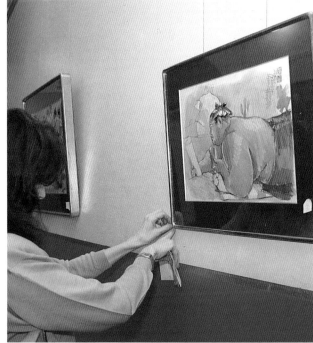

ABOVE: Bridging cultures. Akebono (*left*) in front of London's Tower Bridge.

ABOVE RIGHT: The art of sumo found many fans in London.

RIGHT: Spot the Beefeater. Akebono and friend in London.

BELOW: No chanko-nabe in London, but Wakahanada (*center*) doesn't seem to mind too much.

SUMO BACKGROUND

Sources of Sumo Information

Sumo: A Pocket Guide by Walter Long, published by Charles E. Tuttle Publishing Co., Inc.
A handy pocket guide to appreciating Japan's most popular traditional sport.

The Joy of Sumo by David Benjamin, published by Charles E. Tuttle Publishing Co., Inc.
An irreverent look at sumo from one of Tokyo's funniest writers.

Other books on sumo are available at the Charles E. Tuttle bookshop.
Kanda Jimbocho 1-3, Chiyoda-ku, Tokyo 101
Tel. (03) 3291-7071

Sumo World magazine, published six times a year, prior to each basho. For worldwide subscription information write to:
Sumo World
Andy Adams
c/o Foreign Press Club, 1-7-1 Yurakucho, Chiyoda-ku, Tokyo 100, Japan
Tel. (03) 3211-3161
Fax. (0422) 47-5715

Where and When to See Sumo

Tokyo Basho (January, May, and September)
Kokugikan, 13-28 Yokoami, Sumida-ku, Tokyo 130
Tel. (03) 3623-5111

Haru Basho (March)
Osaka Furitsu Taiikukan (Osaka Prefectural Gymnasium)
3-4-36 Nanbanaka, Naniwa-ku, Osaka 556
Tel. (06) 631-0120

Nagoya Basho (July)
Aichi Kenritsu Taiikukan (Aichi Prefectural Gymnasium)
1-1 Ninomaru, Naka-ku, Nagoya 460
Tel. 0529-71-0015

Kyushu Basho (November)
Fukuoka Kokusai Sentaa (Fukuoka International Center)
2-2 Chikko Honmachi, Hakata-ku, Fukuoka 812
Tel. 0922-91-9311

Stables

It is possible for visitors to visit the stables to watch the morning practices particularly if a prior appointment has been made.

Azumazeki Beya (Stablemaster Azumazeki Oyakata, Akebono)
4-6-4 Higashi Komagata, Sumida-ku, Tokyo 130
Tel. (03) 3625-0033

Takasago Beya (Konishiki)
1-22-5 Yanagibashi, Taito-ku, Tokyo 111
Tel. (03) 3861-3210

Musashigawa Beya (Musashimaru)
3-2-9 Hirano, Koto-ku, Tokyo 135
Tel. (03) 3641-0947

Fujishima Beya (Takahanada and Wakahanada)
3-10-6 Honcho, Nakano-ku, Tokyo 164
Tel. (03) 3375-0391

Sumo Divisions

There are six divisions in sumo (not including the *mae-zumo*, pre-sumo, not listed in the official rankings), the members of which generally change through promotion and demotion after each basho. The divisions, from bottom to top, are as follow:

Jonokuchi: No fixed number of members. Apprentice rikishi.
Jonidan: No fixed number of members. Apprentice rikishi.
Sandanme: Approximately two hundred. Apprentice rikishi.
Makushita: Maximum of 120 members. Apprentice rikishi.
Juryo: Maximum of twenty-six members. Full-fledged sekitori.
Makunouchi: Maximum of thirty-eight members. Full-fledged sekitori.

Within the top, *Makunouchi* division the rankings, from bottom to top, are as follow:

Maegashira: Usually twenty-eight to thirty-one in each basho, but this is not fixed.
Komusubi: Never less than two in each basho.
Sekiwake: Never less than two in each basho.
Ozeki: Usually between two and five in each tournament.
Yokozuna: At the time of writing, no rikishi held this rank, from which there can be no demotion.

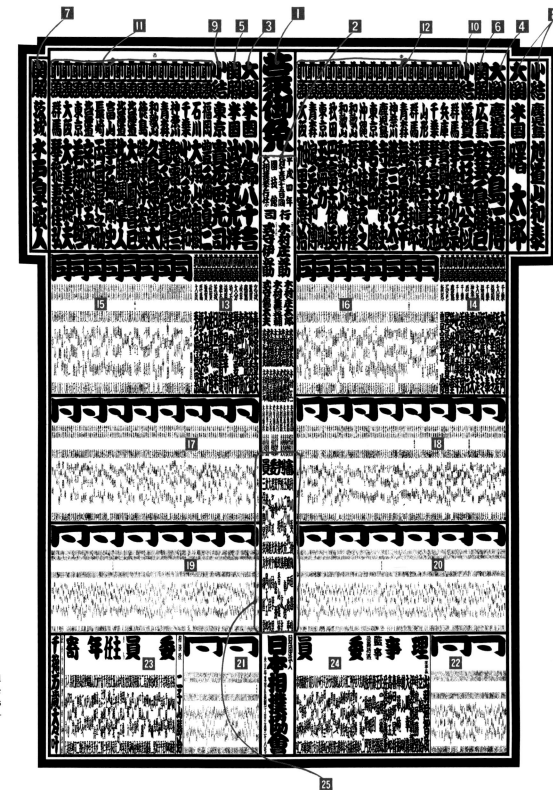

Key:

1. Formal Greeting.
2. Date and place of the basho (September, 1992, at Tokyo's Kokugikan).
3. Nishi (West) ozeki.
4. Higashi (East) ozeki.
5. Nishi sekiwake.
6. Higashi sekiwake.
7. Nishi Haridashi (extra) sekiwake.*
8. Higashi Haridashi.
9. Nishi komusubi.
10. Higashi komusubi.
11. Nishi maegashira.
12. Higashi maegashira.
13. Nishi juryo.
14. Higashi juryo.
15. Nishi makushita.
16. Higashi makushita.
17. Nishi sandanme.
18. Higashi sandanme.
19. Nishi jonidan.
20. Higashi jonidan.
21. Nishi jonokuchi.
22. Higashi jonokuchi.
23. Toshiyori (elders).
24. Toshiyori.
25. Shimpan (judges).

* Usually only two rikishi hold this rank in each basho, so the Haridashi rikishi are the ones over two who scored the lowest in the previous basho.

The **Banzuke** (ranking sheet) is published prior to each tournament and contains all current information about rikishi and tournament officials. In traditional sumo style, the rikishi are divided into two sides, East and West, with the East side being the most prestigious.

USEFUL SUMO WORDS AND PHRASES

banzuke: Official ranking sheets printed for each tournament

basho: Sumo tournament, held on alternate months starting in January.

chankoban: Kitchen duty.

chanko-nabe: A rich stew forming the staple diet of rikishi. There are many different styles, and ingredients at various times can include vegetables, fish, and meat.

chiho basho: The three tournaments held annually outside Tokyo: the Haru (Spring) basho in Osaka, the Nagoya basho, and the Kyushu basho held in the city of Fukuoka.

danpatsu-shiki: The retirement ceremony when the former rikishi's topknot is cut.

dohyo: The sumo ring, treated as hallowed ground.

ginosho: Technique award.

gunbai: The fan or paddle held by the referee.

gyoji: The referee.

hanazumo: A one-day sumo exhibition that does not constitute one of the six annual bashos.

heya: The sumo stable. When combined with a name, the "h" becomes a "b," as in Azumazeki Beya.

higashi (-gawa): The east and most prestigious side of the arena or ring.

honbasho: The six official annual tournaments.

jonidan: The second-lowest division in sumo.

jonokuchi: The lowest division in sumo, for beginners and a few older rikishi who have dropped down the ranks without retiring.

jungyo: A tour consisting of exhibition matches.

juryo: The second-highest division. Juryo wrestlers, along with all makunouchi-division competitors, can be referred to as sekitori.

kachikoshi: A winning record in a tournament. At least eight wins in a fifteen-day tournament, or four wins for jonokuchi and makushita-division rikishi.

kantosho: The Fighting Spirit award.

kesho-mawashi: The decorative aprons worn by wrestlers in the juryo and makunouchi divisions.

kettei-sen: Play-off.

kinboshi: Literally "gold star," an award given to a maegashira who has beaten a yokozuna. It includes a monetary gift.

komusubi: Sumo's fourth-highest rank.

kyokai goaisatu: Formal greeting.

maegashira: Members of the makunouchi division not ranked in sanyaku. Beginners, generally in their first basho.

mae-zumo: Literally "before sumo," in other words, not listed in the banzuke.

makekoshi: A tournament record of more losses than wins.

makunouchi: Sumo's top division.

makushita: Sumo's third-highest division.

masuzeki: The enclosed boxes in the stadium. The traditional place to watch sumo.

mawashi: The belt worn by rikishi.

niramiai: The practice of two rikishi trying to stare each other down before a match.

nishi (-gawa): The west side of the sumo arena or stadium.

oichomage: The ginkgo-leaf-shaped topknot.

oyakata: A sumo elder.

ozeki: Champion. Sumo's second-highest rank.

rikishi: Sumo wrestler.

sandanme: Sumo's third-lowest division.

sanyaku: The four highest ranks in sumo: komusubi, sekiwake, ozeki, and yokozuna.

sansho: Three prizes, given for Technique, Fighting Spirit, and Outstanding Performance.

sekitori: A full-fledged rikishi.

sekiwake: Junior champion. Sumo's third-highest rank.

shinpan: Judge.

shitaku-beya: Dressing room.

shukunsho: Outstanding Performance award.

tachiai: The beginning charge in a sumo match.

Tennoshihai: The Emperor's Cup, the most prestigious prize given to the winner of a tournament.

torikumihyo: The list of bouts for a particular day.

tsukebito: Apprentice(s).

yobidashi: Beckoners.

yokozuna: Grand champion. Sumo's highest rank.

zensho: No losses, with no days absent.

zensho yusho: A perfect score in a tournament, with no losses or absences, and the championship.